YUKON

JANICE PARKER

Weigl

CALGARY

www.weigl.com

Published by Weigl Educational Publishers Limited
6325 – 10 Street SE
Calgary, Alberta, Canada
T2H 2Z9
Web site: http://www.weigl.com
Copyright © 2002 WEIGL EDUCATIONAL PUBLISHERS LIMITED

National Library of Canada Cataloguing in Publication Data
Parker, Janice.
  Yukon

  (Eye on Canada)
  Includes Index
  ISBN 1-896990-96-7 (bound) -- ISBN 1-894705-47-5 (pbk.)

  1. Yukon--Juvenile literature. I. Title. II. Series:
FC4011.2.P37 2001   j971.9'1   C00-910485-5
F1091.4.P37 2001

Printed and bound in Canada
1 2 3 4 5 6 7 8 9 0   05 04 03 02 01

We acknowledge the financial support of the Government of Canada through the Book Publishing Industry Development Program (BPIDP) for our publishing activities.

Photograph Credits

Every reasonable effort has been made to trace ownership and to obtain permission to reprint copyright material. The publishers would be pleased to have any errors or omissions brought to their attention so that they may be corrected in subsequent printings.

Cover: Cathie Archibould; Inside Cover: Territorial Government of the Yukon; Cathie Archibould: pages 4T, 4B, 5, 6MR, 7T, 7B, 9B, 10M, 10B, 11T, 11B, 14B, 15ML, 15BL, 20T, 22B, 23T, 23ML, 25ML, 26T, 26B, 27B; Corbis Corporation: pages 13ML, 14T, 24T, 27T; Corel Corporation: pages 17TL; Lyn Hancock: pages 6T, 8B, 10T, 12T, 12B, 13T, 15BR, 16T, 16B, 20B, 22T, 23B, 24B; Mineral City Enterprises Inc.: page 9T; National Archives of Canada: pages 17B(PA147987), 18T(C39883), 18M(PA53228), 19T(PA202054), 19B(PA113219); Territorial Government of the Yukon: page 21; Tourism Saskatchewan: page 8M; Yukon International Storytelling Festival: page 25B.

Project Coordinator
Jill Foran
Design
Warren Clark
Layout
Bryan Pezzi
Cover Design
Terry Paulhus
Photo Researcher
Joe Nelson

CONTENTS

INTRODUCTION

The Yukon is one of Canada's three territories. It is located in the far northwest of the country, and is home to some of the most beautiful natural scenery in North America. In the Yukon, summer days are long and sunny, and the land is covered in colourful wildflowers. The long hours of summer sunshine in the North has earned the Yukon the nickname "Land of the Midnight Sun."

The Yukon's landscape is both diverse and exciting. The territory is made up of towering mountain ranges, rolling plateaus, wide expanses of **tundra**, and rugged coastal areas. Outdoor enthusiasts from all over the world come to the Yukon to experience its amazing wilderness.

The Yukon is home to vast areas of rugged and untouched beauty.

Whitehorse is the capital city of the Yukon Territory.

The Yukon's nickname, "Land of the Midnight Sun," comes from the fact that above the **Arctic Circle**, the sun shines for most of the day and night during the summer months. During the winter, the sun barely shines at all.

Eighty percent of the Yukon is wilderness area.

The Yukon is roughly triangular in shape. It is bordered by Alaska in the west and southwest, British Columbia in the south, the Northwest Territories in the east, and the Beaufort Sea in the north. The territory includes Herschel Island, which lies just north of the mainland in the Beaufort Sea.

People who wish to drive to the Yukon can take one of the two main highways that run through the territory. The Alaska Highway runs from Dawson Creek, British Columbia, to Whitehorse, and continues on to Delta Junction, Alaska. The Stewart-Cassiar Highway begins near Terrace, British Columbia, and meets up with the Alaska Highway near Watson Lake. Some sections of the Stewart-Cassiar are unpaved.

For those who prefer to fly, the Whitehorse International Airport has daily flights to and from Vancouver, and from the Alaskan cities of Juneau, Anchorage, and Fairbanks.

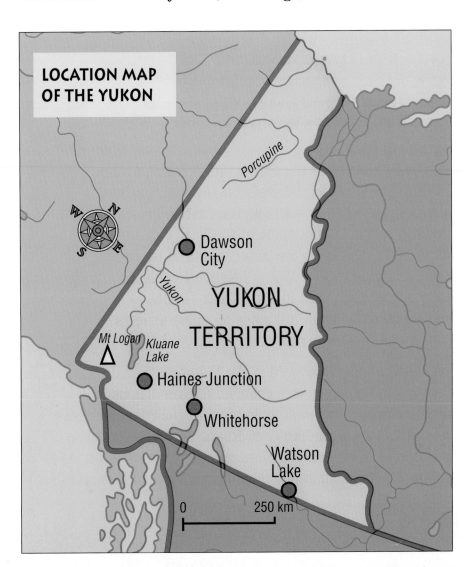

LOCATION MAP OF THE YUKON

Porcupine

Dawson City

Yukon

YUKON TERRITORY

Mt Logan   Kluane Lake

Haines Junction

Whitehorse

Watson Lake

0   250 km

The Yukon Territory was named after the large river running through the region. The Loucheux peoples called the river Yu-kun-ah, which means "Great River." Hudson's Bay Company fur trader John Bell first used the name "Yucon" for the region in 1846. Today, the region is referred to as both "the Yukon" and "Yukon."

The Yukon lies farther west than any other part of Canada.

The Yukon shares more than 1,040 kilometres of border with Alaska.

Herschel Island was named after Sir John Herschel, a well-known chemist and astronomer. The Inuvialuit people who live in the area have always called the island Qikiqtaruk, which means "it is island."

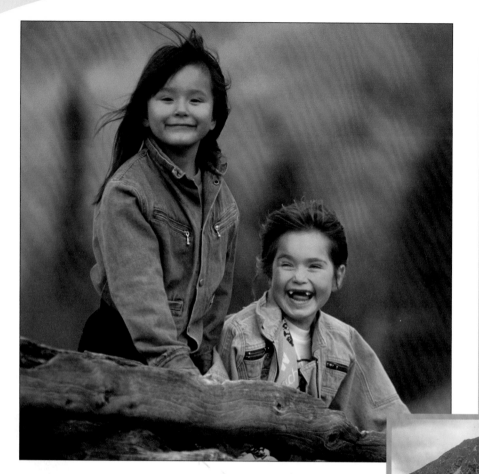

Native Peoples live throughout the Yukon and make up about one-fifth of the territory's population.

The Yukon covers 483,450 square km.

The Yukon is the fifth smallest political region in Canada. Only the four Atlantic provinces—Nova Scotia, Newfoundland, New Brunswick, and Prince Edward Island—are smaller.

The Yukon became a separate territory on June 13th, 1898. Before then, it was part of the Northwest Territories.

There are thirteen lakes in the Yukon. The largest lakes are the Teslin, Kluane, Laberge, Aishihik, and Tagish.

Native Peoples were the earliest inhabitants of the Yukon. They lived in the region many thousands of years ago, and were among the first peoples in North America. Today, some of the Native Peoples who live in the region are descendants of these early inhabitants. The Yukon's Native Peoples have a long and proud history. Their various cultures have a major influence on many aspects of daily life in the territory.

When gold was discovered in the Yukon in the late nineteenth century, the territory was changed forever. Thousands of people came to the area hoping to find their fortune. This was called the **Klondike** Gold Rush. The Gold Rush era resulted in the creation of settlements, roads, businesses, and many colourful stories about the people and events in the region.

Gold was the first important mineral resource discovered in the Yukon. In the twentieth century, other natural resources, such as zinc, lead, and natural gas, became important to the Yukon's economy. As well as the mining industry, tourism is an important source of revenue for the territory. Visitors are drawn to the territory's fascinating historical sites, beautiful natural areas, and exciting cultural festivals.

The national parks, territorial parks, and historic sites in the Yukon are popular destinations. Yukoners and tourists enjoy many outdoor activities, such as snowmobiling, backpacking, and canoeing.

The Yukon River is the second longest in Canada and the fifth longest in North America.

The Arctic Circle goes through the northern part of the Yukon Territory.

There are three National Parks in the Yukon— Ivvavik, Kluane, and Vuntut.

Kluane National Park is a UNESCO World Heritage Site.

The S.S. Klondike National Historic Site in Whitehorse displays one of the largest steamboats used on the Yukon River during the Gold Rush.

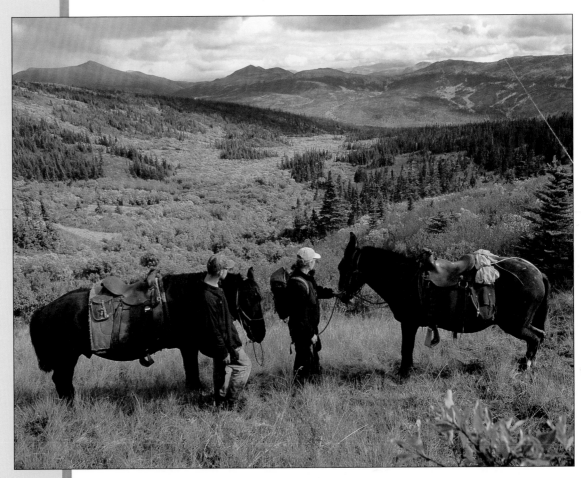

The Yukon's vast wilderness provides an excellent setting for all kinds of outdoor activity.

LAND AND CLIMATE

The Yukon landscape is made up of three main kinds of terrain—mountains, plateaus, and coastal tundra. Most of the territory lies in the Western Cordillera, a great mountain chain that forms the western rim of North America. The Saint Elias mountain range in the southwest is the largest range in the territory. High plateaus separate the mountain ranges, and the area's powerful rivers have carved numerous valleys.

Most of the Yukon is covered by **permafrost**, ground that remains frozen throughout the year. Permafrost lies just beneath a thin upper layer of ground called the active layer. This active layer usually thaws in summer. When the active layer thaws, the frozen ground does not absorb the water, resulting in many swamps and bogs.

The Yukon is situated in the subarctic zone. This means that it is colder than most other regions in Canada. Its summers are short and usually cool, but sometimes temperatures can reach a balmy 25° Celsius. The Yukon's winters are long and cold because the territory is so far north, and the mountains keep the warmer Pacific Ocean air from reaching the region. Winter temperatures in the Yukon usually range from 4°C to –50°C.

The Saint Elias Mountains have vast icefields that are remnants of the last Ice Age.

QUICK FACTS

Canada's highest mountain, Mount Logan, is part of the Saint Elias mountain range. Mount Logan's highest point is 5,959 metres above sea level.

One of the lowest recorded temperatures in North America was recorded in the western Yukon in 1947. It was –63°C.

Because of the darkness, winter in the Yukon is the best time to view the northern lights.

Yukon receives between 23 and 43 centimetres of precipitation each year.

Less than 2 percent of land in the Yukon is suitable for farming.

The official gemstone of the Yukon is lazulite.

Forests cover about 57 percent of the Yukon's total land area.

NATURAL RESOURCES

Ever since gold was first discovered in the territory, the Yukon economy has been centred on its mineral resources. **Prospectors** started the mining industry in the territory when they began digging for gold. After World War II, other minerals, including copper, zinc, lead, silver, and asbestos, began to attract miners. The Yukon is still rich in mineral resources, and mining remains an important activity throughout the territory.

The Yukon's abundance of wildlife was the reason for the territory's thriving fur trade in the 1800s. Today, the territory's animals attract hunters. As well, the many lakes and rivers are full of fish. While there is little commercial fishing in the Yukon, many people fish as a means of obtaining food.

Despite the Yukon's rugged and challenging terrain, mining activity in the territory is abundant. Iron ore is extracted from this open-pit mine near Faro.

PLANTS AND ANIMALS

The Yukon's forests are among the most remote and slowest-growing in the country.

Much of the Yukon is covered in subarctic **boreal forest**, which includes pine, poplar, aspen, and birch trees. Most of the trees and plants in the Yukon are smaller than similar species elsewhere in Canada. They also grow more slowly as a result of the territory's climate. About 1,300 different types of wildflowers, shrubs, and ferns grow in the region. The pasque flower, also called the Yukon crocus, is the first flower to appear through the melting snow in the spring. Blue lupin, Jacob's ladder, arctic poppies, wild roses, and arctic cotton grass are among the many plants that grow in the territory.

In the summer, wild berries provide food for both people and animals. Cranberries, blueberries, strawberries, raspberries, cloudberries, and crowberries are among the many types of edible berries in the Yukon. Bears eat soapberries to fatten up for the winter.

Wild pasque flowers can be seen in the territory. They are regarded as a sign that spring has finally arrived.

QUICK FACTS

The Yukon has over 1,000 species of plants.

Fireweed is the official flower of the territory.

Although trees do not grow above the **tree line**, shrubs and wildflowers are still plentiful.

In coastal areas, which are above the tree line in the Yukon, driftwood is the only wood available for burning and for building.

Forest fires, often started by lightning, destroy millions of square kilometres of forest each year in the Yukon.

A herd of 128,000 barren-ground caribou spend part of the year in the Yukon.

The raven is the Yukon's official bird.

Seals, walruses, and whales live off the Yukon coast.

The Yukon is home to a tremendous variety of animals. Beavers, martens, minks, and arctic and red foxes can all be found in the territory. Wolves, hares, otters, lynxes, wolverines, coyotes, moose, muskoxen, bison, mountain goats, elk, and Dall's sheep also live in the Yukon. All three types of bears common to North America—the American black bear, the grizzly bear, and the polar bear—can be found in the territory.

Many birds spend all or part of the year in the Yukon. Bald eagles, golden eagles, hawks, owls, geese, loons, and ducks all live in the region. Sparrows, ravens, woodpeckers, finches, and jays are also common. The area's lakes, rivers, and seas are home to many different species of fish, including rainbow trout, lake trout, whitefish, arctic char, and several types of salmon.

The Yukon is home to one of North America's largest populations of Dall's sheep. These sheep have a coat that is suited for a cold climate. In the winter, their coats will often grow to more than 5 cm in length.

TOURISM

Tourism is big business in the Yukon. The major tourist season is from late May to late September. During that time, thousands of tourists travel to the Yukon, filling the hotels and keeping the restaurants busy. Many tourism-related businesses are closed for the remainder of the year.

Visitors can learn more about the Yukon's colourful cultural life by exploring the territory's communities. At Whitehorse, a number of museums document every part of the Yukon's past. The Yukon Transportation Museum shows moose-skin boats, snowshoes, stage-coaches, dogsleds, and other early forms of northern transport. The MacBride Museum exhibits the territory's natural and cultural history, and the Old Log Church Museum displays the lives of early missionaries in the north. At Dawson City, a number of historical sites depict the days of the Gold Rush.

The Yukon's many parks provide tourists with excellent opportunities for hiking, mountain climbing, wildlife watching, and other outdoor pursuits. At Kluane National Park, visitors can explore Canada's highest mountains and the largest non-polar icefield in the world.

Kluane National Park is one of the Yukon's most popular natural attractions. The park covers 22,015 sq km of breathtaking wilderness.

QUICK FACTS

The Sign Post Forest in Watson Lake is a collection of more than 40,000 signs. Carl K. Lindley, a homesick Alaskan construction worker, erected the first sign, which pointed to his hometown of Danville, Illinois, in 1942.

The Keno City Mining Museum has artifacts dating back to when Keno City was the largest silver producer in North America.

The Dawson City Museum has many exhibits and artifacts that date back to the height of the Gold Rush.

INDUSTRY

Outfitting and tour companies in the Yukon generate substantial income for the territory every year.

Commercial gardening is an important industry in the Yukon despite the territory's short growing season. Plants in greenhouses grow well during the long daylight hours of the summer months.

There are about 2,100 businesses currently operating in the Yukon.

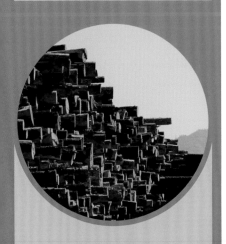

Forestry is becoming an important industry for the Yukon. The territory's high-quality wood is popular around the world.

The mining industry has long been a central part of the Yukon's economy. Mining first became profitable in the territory when the discovery of gold brought thousands of fortune-seekers to the area in the late 1800s. Today, many other minerals are actively explored and mined in the Yukon. Lead, zinc, and silver are all produced at Keno City, near Mayo. These high-grade ores are then transported south to British Columbia for **smelting**. Other resources that hold great future potential for the territory are oil and gas. In 1998, the federal government gave the Yukon government control of the territory's petroleum reserves. There is already one producing gas field in the southeast area of the Yukon.

Tourism is another major industry in the Yukon. It earns the territory around $124 million every year. About 70 percent of the Yukon's working population is employed in jobs related to tourism. Also, the construction of the Alaska Highway during World War II helped make the Yukon more accessible for tourists and contributed to the expansion of many businesses. Then, in 1979, the Canadian government opened the Dempster Highway, east of Dawson City. It was Canada's first all-weather road to cross the Arctic Circle.

GOODS AND SERVICES

Many Yukoners work in one of the territory's manufacturing industries. These industries include mineral refining, printing, and sawmilling. Wood products are among the leading manufactured goods in the Yukon. Locally-made furniture and lumber is sold outside the territory. As well, many local artisans produce beautiful crafts that are sold to the tourists who visit the territory. Some of these goods are also exported to other parts of the world.

The Yukon also produces some farm products, such as livestock, vegetables, and grains. Crops are grown and farm animals are raised mostly for the local market. Fish are important goods for Yukoners. There is some fish processing in the territory, and a small **aquaculture** industry also exists. Like farming, fishing is done mostly for local markets or for personal consumption. Many remote communities in the Yukon rely heavily on fishing, hunting, and trapping for survival.

Yukoner Claire Demarais uses the territory's high-quality wood to build boats.

QUICK FACTS

The Yukon gets most of its energy from two **hydroelectric** facilities.

The Yukon plays a small role in the Canadian fur-production industry.

The Yukon produces about fifteen different newspapers. These include dailies, weeklies, monthlies, and annual publications.

Most employed Yukoners work in one of the territory's many service industries. These are industries that provide some sort of assistance to others. People who work in service industries include administrative assistants, waiters, government workers, and doctors. Many Yukoners work for one of the three levels of government represented in the territory—federal, territorial, or municipal. Other Yukoners work in the retail industry, selling locally-made goods and imports to residents or tourists.

Another important service is education. Although it is a territory rather than a province, the Yukon is still responsible for its own education system. Public school education is administered by four regional superintendents, and there are twenty-eight schools in the territory. Yukon College, a junior college based in Whitehorse, is the only post-secondary school in the territory. The college offers a variety of programs and has campuses in other communities.

Almost one-third of all retail spending in the Yukon is in grocery stories.

The Yukon has five radio stations and two television stations.

The Royal Canadian Mounted Police maintain law and order in the territory.

Stores like this one in Dawson City provide Yukoners and visitors with all kinds of supplies and momentos.

Yukon College's main campus is located at Yukon Place, in Whitehorse.

FIRST NATIONS

Anthropologists estimate there were anywhere from 6,000 to 40,000 Native Peoples living in the Yukon region prior to European settlement. These peoples spoke languages from two main language groups: the Athapaskan group and the Tlingit. There were five major groups of Athapaskans: the Gwich'in, Han, Tutchone, Kaska, and Tagish. Each group lived in a different part of the Yukon. In the 1800s, a group of First Nations from Alaska, the Tlingit, moved into southern Yukon.

The early Native Peoples of the Yukon lived in small groups of twenty to twenty-five people. In order to survive in their harsh environment, they had to work together. They caught fish during the summer, drying much of it for use during the cold winter months. They also gathered berries and hunted small mammals, such as hares. In the fall, they would hunt larger animals, like caribou. In the wintertime, they lived near lakes, catching small mammals and fishing through holes they made in the ice.

Today, many Native Peoples in the Yukon work to preserve the traditional ways of their ancestors through language, music, and art.

QUICK FACTS

Many thousands of years ago, Russia and Alaska were connected by a land bridge. Hunters made use of this land bridge while following bison and woolly mammoth from Asia, through Alaska, to the Yukon.

Early Native Peoples made use of all parts of the animals they hunted. The hides were tanned and used to make clothing. Other body parts were used to make snowshoes and tools. Any leftover meat was smoked to preserve it for later use.

About 500 western Arctic Inuit—called Inuvialuit—lived on the coast around 1890. By the 1920s, most of the Yukon Inuvialuit were either dead from diseases carried by whalers from the United States, or had moved eastward in Canada.

At the end of the nineteenth century, some seamen hunted whales along the north coast, but they did not settle in the area.

The British Navy mapped most of the Arctic islands and straits while searching for John Franklin and his crew.

Reverend Robert McDonald, who came to the Yukon in 1862 and stayed for forty years, translated the Bible into the Gwich'in language.

When Russia sold Alaska to the United States in 1867, the Americans claimed that Fort Yukon was in U.S. territory. The Fort was moved further inland, but later abandoned.

EXPLORERS

European explorers did not arrive in the Yukon area until the first half of the nineteenth century. Many entered the region while searching for the Northwest Passage, a short-cut trading route linking the Atlantic and Pacific Oceans. Sir John Franklin, a British sea captain, was among the most famous of these explorers. He and his crew were probably the first to reach the Yukon region when they visited Herschel Island in 1825. Franklin made three trips to explore the Arctic.

In the 1840s, the Hudson's Bay Company sent people to the Yukon to establish the fur trade in the region. John Bell explored the Yukon interior via the Porcupine and Yukon Rivers, and Robert Campbell sailed westward from the Mackenzie River system to explore the Pelly River. In 1848, Campbell established a fur trading post at Fort Selkirk, near the junction of the Yukon and Pelly Rivers. Other posts, including Fort Frances and Fort Yukon, were also set up during the 1840s. However, the fur trade in the Yukon was not a huge success. The region was too remote, and transporting furs to Britain took a great deal of time and trouble. Trading posts were often abandoned just a few years after being established.

On his third trip to the Arctic, in 1845, John Franklin and his men died tragically when their ships became stuck in the icy waters.

EARLY SETTLERS

Several gold-mining centres were set up in the Yukon during the late nineteenth century. Many of these centres lasted only a brief period as prospectors and businesspeople moved through the area in search of gold.

In the 1860s, Britain bought the Yukon back from the Hudson's Bay Company. The British feared that the United States might try to take control of the area, and they wanted to prevent this from happening. Canada became an independent nation in 1867, and the Yukon became part of the Northwest Territories in 1895. At that time, there were only about 1,000 people living in the region.

Early gold prospectors moved into the area in the 1860s and 1870s. Some gold was found during those years, but not enough to generate worldwide interest. In 1896, an enormous amount of gold was discovered in the Klondike River and the Gold Rush began. By 1898, up to 100,000 people came from across North America and Europe in the hope of finding their fortune in the north. The North-West Mounted Police required that each prospector going through the Chilkoot Pass have enough supplies to last one year in the wilderness. This amounted to about 800 kilograms of supplies. Prospectors had to make several trips through the pass to carry their supplies.

QUICK FACTS

Before 1896, most of the residents of the Yukon were First Nations peoples.

Gold was discovered in a tributary of the Klondike River in August 1896, making the Yukon famous around the world.

Skookum Jim, Tagish Charlie, and George Carmack are all credited with finding the gold that began the Klondike Gold Rush.

Prior to the Gold Rush, Dawson City was home to very few people. In May 1898, it became the largest city in North America west of Winnipeg and north of San Francisco. About 40,000 people lived in the city, and many hotels, casinos, saloons, and dance halls opened. The Klondike Gold Rush was instrumental in developing the Yukon. The White Pass and Yukon Railway was created to help people travel to the region.

The Yukon remained a fairly peaceful region during the Gold Rush thanks to the work of the North-West Mounted Police.

In 1900, a railway was built between Whitehorse and Skagway, Alaska.

At the height of the Klondike Gold Rush, Dawson City was known as "Paris North."

The Yukon became a separate territory on June 13, 1898. It was established to help protect Canadian land from the flood of American prospectors during the Gold Rush.

After the Gold Rush died down, the population of the Yukon decreased quickly. The construction of the Alaska Highway during World War II again brought people to the area. Thousands of Canadian and American construction workers came to help build the highway. Businesses sprung up to provide services to the workers. Whitehorse, which is on the Alaska Highway route, became the largest community in the territory.

Once construction of the Alaska Highway was completed, access to the Yukon became much more convenient.

POPULATION

Whitehorse is the transportation, communication, and distribution centre of the Yukon.

The Yukon has a population of about 31,000. About two-thirds of these people live in the territory's only city—Whitehorse. Other Yukoners live in Dawson City, Watson Lake, or Haines Junction, which are the only three towns in the territory. The Yukon also has four villages, thirteen unincorporated communities, and eight rural communities. Much of the territory remains unpopulated.

Most Yukoners come from other parts of Canada. Many of these people come to the Yukon because of the high wages. They often plan to stay in the territory for only a short time to make money. Nearly half of the Yukon's people have some British ancestry, and about 21 percent have Native ancestry.

POLITICS AND GOVERNMENT

The Yukon's territorial government meets at the Legislative Building in Whitehorse.

The Yukon has had elected representatives in the territorial government since 1900.

The Yukon Progressive Conservative Party was the first political party elected to run the territorial government.

In 1991, the Yukon Progressive Conservative Party, who wanted to set themselves apart from the federal PC party, became the Yukon Party. Today, the Yukon Party, the Yukon Liberal Party, and the Yukon New Democratic Party are the three major political parties in the territory.

The Yukon Territory elects one member to the federal Parliament in Ottawa. The member of Parliament (MP) serves a term of up to five years. One senator represents the Yukon in parliament.

The Yukon territorial government consists of three separate bodies. A Legislative Assembly, consisting of seventeen elected members, governs the Yukon Territory. The main executive body is the Cabinet, or executive council, made up of members of the Legislative Assembly. A premier is the head of the Cabinet. All members of the Legislative Assembly are elected to four-year terms.

The judicial branch of government includes the court of appeal, which is the territory's highest court and hears appeals from lower courts. The Supreme Court hears major civil and criminal cases and is made up of two resident and forty nonresident justices. The Yukon territorial court has three resident and fourteen nonresident judges.

The Yukon's local government is much the same as local governments throughout the country. A mayor and council run the towns and Whitehorse. The federal government appoints a commissioner to be in charge of federal interests in the territory.

CULTURAL GROUPS

Native Peoples have contributed greatly to the Yukon's cultural atmosphere. Numerous museums, festivals, and other cultural events help to keep Native cultures alive in the territory. Artwork, music, storytelling, and poems are just a few of the important cultural expressions of the Yukon's Native Peoples.

Throughout their history, the Native Peoples of the Yukon have developed beautiful artwork and crafts. Early clothing was decorated with items such as beads, porcupine quills, seeds, and moose hair. The Yukon's Native Peoples also had a tradition of carving crests and images of the animals representing different groups. These images were embroidered on clothes and painted on walls, boats, and drums. Today, many Native artists make carvings from antlers and other animal bones. They also make jewellery, moccasins, masks, beadwork, and paintings.

The Yukon's beautiful scenery and rich traditions have inspired many artists in the territory. Expressions of the Yukon's natural and cultural heritage are found in carvings, jewellery, paintings, and craftwork.

QUICK FACTS

Many of the Yukon's Native Peoples are skilled in unique craftmaking. *Qiviuq* is the craft of spinning wool from the underhair of a muskox. Caribou tufting is the shaping of caribou hair into designs and sewing the tufts of hair onto fabric as decoration.

Today, the Yukon has fourteen Native groups. Eight different traditional languages are spoken in the territory—seven Athapaskan languages and one Tlingit.

Dawson City was made a National Historic Site because of the lively and important role it played in the territory's history.

The **potlatch** is a festive Native ceremony involving dancing, feasting, and the giving of gifts.

Early missionaries to the Yukon felt that the potlatch was an evil celebration. The Canadian government made potlatches illegal in 1884. In 1951, the government declared that potlatches were no longer illegal. Native Peoples in the Yukon continue to hold potlatches today.

The Yukon Sourdough Rendezvous is celebrated each February in Whitehorse. The festival is a celebration of the nearing of the end of winter. People dress in costumes from the beginning of the twentieth century. Sled dog races, fiddle contests, and dances are among the events.

Different museums and festivals in the Yukon celebrate other aspects of the territory's rich history. The Gold Rush was the single most important event in the history of the Yukon. Many museums and annual festivals celebrate the customs of the Gold Rush era. Visitors can learn how gold was panned at several places in the Yukon. The Klondike Visitors Association has a site on Bonanza Creek, where the Gold Rush first began. Panning involves scooping up gravel from the bottom of a stream in a large metal pan. After rotating the pan underwater for several minutes, the gravel is drained off. Any pieces of heavy gold sink to the bottom of the pan.

Visitors interested in panning for gold are still likely to find gold flakes and nuggets among the gravel from the territory's creeks.

The Yukon also holds a number of festivals related to the Klondike Gold Rush. One of the most popular is Discovery Days, held every August in Dawson City. Festivities include a parade, huge picnics, and raft races.

Visitors to Bonanza Creek can learn more about the area's Gold Rush by taking part in traditional panning and gold-seeking methods.

ARTS AND ENTERTAINMENT

The Yukon has inspired several talented writers. Among the most prominent writers who have lived in the area are Robert Service and Jack London. In 1894, at the age of 20, Robert Service moved from England to Canada. He lived in Dawson City at the height of the Gold Rush. He captured the experience of the era in his poems and stories. "The Shooting of Dan McGrew" was about a real-life shootout in a Whitehorse saloon. Today, Service's cabin in Dawson City is a tourist spot. American writer Jack London also lived in the area during the Gold Rush. His experiences in the north inspired some of his writing, including one of his most famous books, *The Call of the Wild*.

One of Canada's most prominent and respected writers, Pierre Berton, is from the Yukon. Born in Whitehorse, he grew up in the territory, and has written many books about the area including the well-received *Klondike*. In 1986, Berton was named Companion to the Order of Canada.

Robert Service's cabin is now part of the Dawson Historical Complex. Visitors to the cabin have the pleasure of listening to recitals of Service's poems and stories, which are performed daily.

The Yukon has a number of popular music festivals that draw large crowds. The Frostbite Music Festival is held every February in Whitehorse. This festival combines lively concerts with dances, workshops, and children's activities to create a memorable experience for anyone who attends. The concerts feature both northern performers and other Canadian musicians. Later in the year, the Alsek Music Festival greets summer at Kluane National Park. Yukon musicians and audiences sing and dance within the beautiful mountain setting. Then, in July, the Dawson City Music Festival runs for three days under a sun that never sets. The festival has attracted talented musicians and is known nationally as "Canada's tiny, perfect festival."

Storytelling is another art form that exists throughout the territory. The Yukon International Storytelling Festival has been held every year since 1988. Yukon Native storytellers are joined by storytellers from around the world who speak many different languages.

Artist Ted Harrison was born in England but spent many years in the Yukon. His bright paintings of the Yukon people and landscape have made him one of Canada's most beloved artists.

Yukoners who are interested in live theatre can take in a show at Whitehorse's Nakai Theatre or Dawson City's Palace Grand Theatre.

A famous show called *The Gaslight Follies* is performed at the Palace Grand Theatre. It consists of two hours of musical comedy centred around the Klondike Gold Rush.

Performers at the Yukon International Storytelling Festival captivate audiences with creative forms of storytelling.

SPORTS

The wide expanses of land and diverse landscapes of the Yukon make the territory a perfect spot for many different activities. A variety of outdoor recreation is popular in the region. Many people fish, canoe, and boat in Yukon waters. Others hunt the big game that roam the territory's mountain wilderness. The Yukon also has excellent backpacking, hiking, camping, and horseback riding opportunities. Adventurous people participate in mountain biking, white-water rafting, river rafting and mountain climbing.

In the winter, cross-country skiing, snowshoeing, snowmobiling, and skating are all popular pastimes. Organized sports in the territory include hockey, curling, soccer, golf, volleyball, and tennis.

Kayak and canoe enthusiasts demonstrate their skills at Whitehorse's annual Whitewater Rodeo.

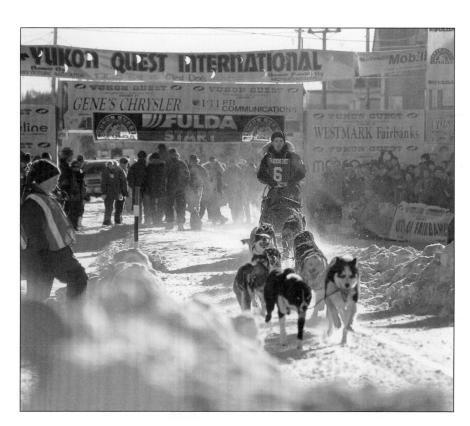

Every January, athletes compete in the Alcan 200 International Snowmachine Race, which runs through Alaska and the Yukon. Racers travel at speeds over 160 km per hour over a 296-km route. This is considered the world's longest snowmachine race.

The Klondike Trail of 1898 International Road Relay is a foot-race over 176 km. Ten team members run different stages over a variety of terrain.

The Great Klondike International Outhouse Race has been held every year since 1977 in Dawson City. Teams made up of five contestants, one sitting inside the outhouse and four carrying it, see who can complete the 3-km course first. Competitors usually take turns sitting in the outhouse to get a rest during the race.

Dogsled racing is a popular sport in the territory's northern regions. The Yukon Quest is considered one of the most difficult sled dog races in the world. The race takes place between Whitehorse and Fairbanks, Alaska, every February. Fifty teams from around the world come to compete in the race. Teams have eight to fourteen dogs and only one **musher**. Many different dog breeds are used, but Siberian huskies, malamutes, and husky-shepherd crosses are the most common. It takes about ten to fourteen days to finish the race, but each team is required to take a 36-hour break in Dawson City. The freezing temperatures of the north make the race even harder. Sometimes temperatures can drop to as low as –62°C.

The Yukon Quest begins in Whitehorse in odd-numbered years and in Fairbanks during even-numbered years. However, in 1998, the race began in Whitehorse to commemorate the **centennial** of the 1898 Klondike Gold Rush.

Competitors in the Yukon Quest must travel 1,600 km of difficult terrain during the coldest month of the year.

EYE ON CANADA

The Yukon is one of the ten provinces and three territories that make up Canada. Compare the Yukon's statistics with those of other provinces and territories. What differences and similarities can you find?

Northwest Territories

Entered Confederation:
July 15, 1870

Capital: Yellowknife

Area: 171,918 sq km

Population: 41,606
Rural: 58 percent
Urban: 42 percent

Population Density:
0.24 people per sq km

Yukon

Entered Confederation:
June 13, 1898

Capital: Whitehorse

Area: 483,450 sq km

Population: 30,633
Rural: 40 percent
Urban: 60 percent

Population Density:
0.06 people
per sq km

British Columbia

Entered Confederation:
July 20, 1871

Capital: Victoria

Area: 947,800 sq km

Population: 4,023,100
Rural: 18 percent
Urban: 82 percent

Population Density:
4.24 people
per sq km

Alberta

Entered Confederation:
September 1, 1905

Capital: Edmonton

Area: 661,190 sq km

Population: 2,964,689
Rural: 20 percent
Urban: 80 percent

Population Density:
4.48 people
per sq km

Saskatchewan

Entered Confederation:
September 1, 1905

Capital: Regina

Area: 652,330 sq km

Population: 1,027,780
Rural: 28 percent
Urban: 72 percent

Population Density:
1.57 people per sq km

Manitoba

Entered Confederation:
July 15, 1870

Capital: Winnipeg

Area: 649,950 sq km

Population: 1,143,509
Rural: 28 percent
Urban: 72 percent

Population Density:
1.76 people per sq km

250   500 km

Nunavut

Entered Confederation:
April 1, 1999

Capital: Iqaluit

Area: 1,900,000 sq km

Population: 27,039

Population Density:
0.014 people per sq km

Quebec

Entered Confederation:
July 1, 1867

Capital: Quebec City

Area: 1,540,680 sq km

Population: 7,345,390
Rural: 21 percent
Urban: 79 percent

Population Density:
4.77 people per sq km

CANADA

Confederation:
July 1,1867

Capital: Ottawa

Area: 9,203,054 sq km

Population: 30,491,294
Rural: 22 percent
Urban: 78 percent

Population Density:
3.06 people
per sq km

Newfoundland & Labrador

Entered Confederation:
March 31, 1949

Capital: St. John's

Area: 405,720 sq km

Population: 541,000
Rural: 43 percent
Urban: 57 percent

Population Density:
1.33 people
per sq km

Prince Edward Island

Entered Confederation:
July 1, 1873

Capital:
Charlottetown

Area: 5,660 sq km

Population: 137,980
Rural: 56 percent
Urban: 44 percent

Population Density:
24.38 people
per sq km

Nova Scotia

Entered Confederation:
July 1, 1867

Capital: Halifax

Area: 55,490 sq km

Population: 939,791
Rural: 45 percent
Urban: 55 percent

Population Density:
16.94 people
per sq km

Ontario

Entered Confederation:
July 1, 1867

Capital: Toronto

Area: 1,068,580 sq km

Population: 11,513,808
Rural: 17 percent
Urban: 83 percent

Population Density:
10.77 people per sq km

New Brunswick

Entered Confederation:
July 1, 1867

Capital: Fredericton

Area: 73,440 sq km

Population: 754,969
Rural: 51 percent
Urban: 49 percent

Population Density:
10.28 people per sq km

BRAIN TEASERS

Test your knowledge of the Yukon by trying to answer these mind-boggling brain teasers!

1 Make a Guess:

How did the city of Whitehorse get its name?

2 True or False:

Whitehorse is the most westerly community in Canada.

3 Multiple Choice:

What proportion of the surface area in Kluane National Park is covered in ice?

a. 22 percent
b. 82 percent
c. 100 percent
d. 46 percent

4 True or False:

Mount Logan, in Kluane National Park, is considered to be the world's most massive block of rock.

5 True or False:

The northernmost highway in the world runs through the Yukon.

6 True or False:

The world's largest weather vane is at the Whitehorse International Airport.

7 Make a Guess:

What community was the capital of the Yukon before Whitehorse was made capital in 1953?

8 Multiple Choice:

Which of the following Yukon communities is the smallest?

a. Dawson City
b. Whitehorse
c. Watson Lake
d. Faro

1. The name originated from the prospectors heading to the Klondike in 1898. They thought that the rapids of the Yukon River near the area resembled the mane of a white horse.

2. False: Whitehorse is the most westerly city, but Beaver Creek is the most westerly community in Canada. Both, however, are located in the Yukon.

3. b. 82 percent

4. True.

5. True. The Dempster Highway runs through the Yukon and continues north to Inuvik in the Northwest Territories.

6. True. It is made from a DC-3 airplane.

7. Dawson City.

8. d. Faro.

GLOSSARY

aquaculture: fish farming

Arctic Circle: the line of latitude running through the northern hemisphere at about 66°33' North

boreal forest: a large area in the northern hemisphere covered mainly in trees including pine, spruce, fir, birch, and poplar

centennial: a 100th anniversary

hydroelectric: electricity generated by moving water

Klondike: a region of the Yukon Territory near the Klondike River

musher: a person who navigates dog sleds

permafrost: permanently frozen ground

potlatch: a celebration held by certain North American First Nations groups. Depending on the group, potlatches may be held to celebrate marriages or deaths.

prospectors: people who explore a region for precious minerals such as gold

smelting: melting ore to obtain metal

tree line: a line of latitude and altitude beyond which trees will not grow

tundra: an Arctic or subarctic plain with a permanently frozen subsoil

BOOKS

Hancock, Lyn. *Yukon* (Hello Canada). Minneapolis, Minnesota: Lerner Publications Company, 1996.

Tempelman-Kluit, Anne. *Yukon* (Discover Canada). Toronto: Grolier Limited, 1994.

Zuehlke, Mark. *The Yukon Fact Book*. Vancouver: Whitecap Books, 1998.

WEB SITES

The Yukon government
http://www.gov.yk.ca
Touring the Yukon
http://www.touryukon.com
Yukon Web
http://www.yukonweb.com

Some Web sites stay current longer than others. To find information on the Yukon, use your Internet search engine to look up such topics as "Whitehorse," "Klondike," "Dawson City," or any other topic you wish to research.

INDEX